BUSINESS SUCCESS PATHWAYS

BAMIDELE OYENOWO DANIEL

DEDICATION

This book is dedicated to all beginners and tycoons in business around the world.

CONTENTS

INTRODUCTION

Making quality profits, gaining new clients, the ability to keep them, your customers been your brand ambassadors are all part of business success. Most companies and individuals find it as a bone in the throat to keep their existing customers and also to gain new ones. It is never a good testimony for your customer(s) to settle for another product.

'Business Success pathways ' is a detailed book that maximize your chances of gaining new customers and magnetizing them. It includes a step by step guide to business success via practicing of new strategies that suits your brand policy.

Customers are the best advertisers!

CHAPTER ONE

Gaining new customers

....the new bees

It's pretty obvious that without customers, you don't have a business. But attracting new customers doesn't happen automatically. You have to find ways to reach them, draw them in, and keep them coming back for more. Your business needs a marketing plan that addresses how to attract customers and increase sales.

A "marketing plan" can sound a little intimidating, but

don't worry! The good news is you don't need a team of MBAs to bring in new customers. These 5 affordable, easy-to-implement strategies will help you build a marketing plan that works for your business.

Figuring out how to attract customers is a matter of a bit of PR savvy, common sense, and some tactical business moves. It's also a matter of elbow grease – keeping up with email campaigns, social media, and review sites takes work. Budgeting for promotions and samples takes work, too. But all of that will pay off as your customer base grows. Just remember to be flexible – try things out and see what works for your business. When you hit on a winning strategy, your bottom line will show it.

Most entrepreneurs started their businesses because they love the work they do, not because they like selling. Unfortunately, your business won't survive if you're not good at attracting new customers.

As a small business owner, you're always on the hunt for new customers — that's the name of the game, after all! Even if you've built up a loyal core customer base, new customers are key to scaling your business for the long term. The fact is, repeat customers can either move away or fall on hard times and do less discretionary spending.

You need to make sure your business is always relevant and inviting to new customers and clients. The influx of different customers helps you keep customer service solid and your business and products innovative. New people keep you on your toes and they bring in new sources of revenue for the business. If revenue is starting to slow or get stagnant, it's time for you to come up with some new and creative ways to market your business to new customers.

Success is all about me.

Significance is all about we

.....Kris Denbesten

STRATEGIES TO GAIN NEW CUSTOMERS

1. Identify Your Ideal New Customers

One of the most common tenets of any effective sales marketing campaign is knowing the customer. The first question is, "Who is your ideal new customer?" The second question is, "What does your ideal new customer want from your business?"

It's far easier to develop an effective marketing strategy for one person than for every person – not every person will want the exact same thing, so you have to cast a huge net to draw mass attention. Some giant corporations can do that – Amazon, for example, or Target. They have the infrastructure and market power to pull customers from nearly every demographic. But even those giant companies put special emphasis on certain demographics that are likely to be good customers. So, the first step is to clearly define your client base.

This step will take some internet research, getting out there and talking to different demographics, and some good old-fashioned brainstorming. Think about the kinds of people that will be attracted to your product or service. You can start with really general categories – does your business cater toward men, women, or both, for example. You can also break it down by age, income, and location, to name a few. The trick is to get to a target that's specific enough to be worth targeting but not so specific that you're cutting out potential customers.

For example, contrast two niche groups: "women aged 30-50" versus "women aged 30-50 who like yoga, own dogs, and live within 10 miles of our shop." See how much easier it would be to craft a specific target message to the latter group? Maybe you're selling athletic wear – you could set up a Twilight Yoga and Yappy Hour (e.g, bring your dogs) event at a local dog park to entice new customers to try your products. The more you know about your customer, the happier you can make them with your direct, just for them (or so it seems!) marketing, events, and products.

2. Use Direct Response Marketing to Attract Customers

Direct response marketing is a popular tactic where you ask your customers to engage in a call to action; usually, this involves responding to an email or opting into your email marketing group. The benefit of this type of marketing is that you're creating a roster of interested customers that you can reach out to with sales, events, newsletters, and other reminders to keep your brand in the front of their minds.

Direct marketing works best when you craft intriguing compelling messages designed to attract customers and pique their collective interest. Some brands do it by offering rewards for signing up. For example, say you're running a bakery. You could allow people to enter a drawing for a free cake in exchange for signing up for your newsletter. Others offer a discount on the next purchase after signing up for the email list, and still others simply heavily emphasize their email marketing and frequently prompt people to sign up. Make sure to include calls to action on your website and in your brick-and-mortar store – let people know that they might be missing out on great opportunities with your business.

Of course, in order to attract new customers and increase sales, you'll have to actually keep up with the emails. Send out regular newsletters with updates about new products, promotions, news about your business, and whatever else your customers may want to know. As with any marketing materials, make sure your newsletter fits your brand – the same logo, messaging, and tone as you use online and in-store. You can use a service like MailChimp to customize a design template and send emails to your whole list at once, which makes it look professional.

3. Give Something Away to Entice New Customers

Handing out free stuff may not seem like the most logical business plan for a small business, especially when you're starting out on a lean budget. But this is one instance when it pays to sink a little upfront money into making more money later.

Giving away free or discounted products can bring customers through your doors. For example, you can offer a discount for first-time customers – maybe they get 10% off on their first purchase. You can also offer incentives for your current customers to refer new customers – like offering them $5 off for every new customer they bring in. Then you have new customers coming in and your original customer will come back to take advantage of the discount. It's worth shaving off that $5 to increase sales overall.

Some business experts recommend pairing with a partner to offer a free product. For example, a tax prep company can pair with a computer store to offer an hour of free service. A salon can offer free travel-sized hair products or a certificate for discounts on future salon services for those who spend a certain amount at a neighboring boutique. The key to making this tactic work is to align with a prospective partner who shares the same ideal niche customer.

4. Give Your Business a Face Lift to Increase Sales

If your business is housed in a brick-and-mortar shop, then it's important to pay attention to the message the exterior of your shop sends to those passing by. Does it fit your brand? Does it fit the area? Is it in good shape or does it look like it's falling apart?

You want your business to put its best foot forward right from the start. Rather than neglecting your storefront, give it a critical look and assess your shop as though you were a brand-new customer. Is it clean and well-lit? Is your signage in good shape? Is it visible from the road? By the same token, the inside of your shop should be clean, in good repair, and designed to fit your brand's image and your target customers' tastes. You should also consider the physical layout – is it easy for customers to move through the shop? Are there bottlenecks or cramped areas that you could rearrange? Maybe you can move displays around to make it easy for customers to linger a little longer and see a few more of your products as they move through the store.

The same is true of online businesses. Try to put yourself in your customer's shoes and take a look at your website. Does it look professional? Does it fit your brand, with appropriate logos and messaging? Once you're past the immediate aesthetics, make sure the site works. Every link should take you to the right place, all of the information should be correct, and the shopping and payment mechanisms should work smoothly. It should also be easy to use – you want it to be as simple as possible to get from shopping to checkout.

Making your business look good is a great way to increase sales, with the added benefit of pleasing your current customers.

5. Get The (Right) Word Out

Above all, the best thing you can do to attract new customers is to spread the word as far and wide as possible about your business. Depending on your target demographic, that may mean advertising online, in newspapers, or even on billboards. If your budget is too tight for that kind of expenditure, social media offers a great way to reach lots of consumers for free.

These days, word-of-mouth advertising is really word-of-internet. Reach out to your personal social networks and let them know about your business. Ask them to follow your business on social media and spread the word to their friends and beyond. Keep up an active social media presence and use it to stay in touch with your customers.

In a similar vein, keep an eye on review sites like Yelp. Encourage your customers to leave good reviews to boost your ratings. You should also address any negative reviews; that may involve apologizing or offering a refund or a free product or service as compensation. That shows them and everyone else on the site that you care about your customers.

The first step to drawing a new customer in is simply making sure they know your business exists. Everything else follows from there.

CHAPTER TWO

Customers Engagement

...be their attention

Customer engagement benefits buyers and suppliers alike by increasing close rates while meeting current B2B customer expectations. Keep customers engaged throughout their purchase journey to develop customer loyalty and collect valuable customer information.

More customer interactions lead buyers to find your brand more valuable and provide you with customer insights. Those customer insights can inform marketing decisions such as retargeting and content development, as well as sales processes such as messaging and outreach methods.

Having engaged customers are much more likely to feel a connection with your brand and therefore purchase and return to purchase. The moments and interactions on your website all play a part in the buyer's journey and the final sales completion.

HOW TO IGNITE CUSTOMER ENGAGEMENT

Create an effective engagement marketing strategy.

A marketing engagement strategy should heavily consider what existing and potential customers need throughout their purchase journey. Identify the key steps in your target audience's purchase journey and add a touchpoint to reach customers consistently. Each touchpoint should include helpful, personalized information to provide positive customer experience and build customer loyalty. Develop content that supports buyers' evolving needs throughout the funnel. Use customer insight and data to create a positive brand perception and boost engagement across all channels. Create content that is relevant, as well as resourceful, and helps your target buyer understand how your solution will help them solve their business challenges. Think strategically about what should be included in marketing content, the appropriate outreach channel and how it may affect your customer interactions.

Boost sales success with customer engagement.

Build trust between your sales team and customers through consistent, personalized touchpoints on a variety of relevant channels. Remember that each touch should meet the customer's progress along their purchase journey, and provide useful information or content that drives their movement through the sales funnel. Supply your sales teams with customer interaction insights, which they can use to develop thoughtful messaging and select content that supports specific outreach goals.

Sales interactions should support customers as they research and narrow their options, but shouldn't feel forced. Be perceptive when interacting with customers, take note of what works, and find the channels and types of outreach that work best for your team and ideal buyer persona. When you strive to improve connections and lead handoffs between sales and marketing, customer engagement is essential. Marketers should deliver timely, personalized content that educates and creates qualified leads. Sales should continue to nurture and engage buyers across a variety of channels to establish business relationships and increase close rates.

Increased brand visibility

Word-of-mouth marketing carried out by a satisfied customer is one of the most powerful ways to increase brand visibility.

There's a strong link between happy, engaged customers and repeat business. A loyal consumer will demonstrate their devotion to your brand by purchasing from you again, talking positively about you online, and engaging in brand advocacy. If you can successfully engage your customers, they'll continue to keep your brand at the forefront of your mind. It will also increase their receptivity to your advertising messages.

CHAPTER THREE

Online customer engagement

...the internet ways

Online customer engagement is more than just clicks and conversions, it's the moments between. Successful customer engagement creates a positive experience and keeps your brand at the top of the customer's mind during the consideration phase of the buyer's journey.

Furthermore, great online engagement also makes your marketing campaigns more effective. The way social media works, for example, means that the more engagement and interactions you get, the more impressions and visability you get.

Online customer engagement is important for your bottom line and revenue but also to have more positive marketing outcomes to enable you to build material for the future.

Get creative with customer engagement, especially on social media, and don't limit outreach and marketing campaigns to only Twitter and Facebook. For example, does your target audience include a younger demographic? Consider newer social platforms such as TikTok. Or would your product benefit from a visual aid or experience? Add Instagram to the planned engagement mix.

Marketing is about selling. This has been the truth for

decades, and it still holds true today. Businesses have always used special deals and offers to entice people to buy. But now, actively engaging with customers is also an important part of the process.It wasn't always possible to communicate with customers in a non-sales context. Even phone calls and letters had to be framed around making sales.

It's no secret that consumers are evolving rapidly. They have become more demanding, impatient, and at the end of the day, quite spoiled for choice. This means businesses have to fight more than ever before to capture their attention online. But just sparking an interest isn't enough, you need to be able to provide authentic content that engages and delights them. If done successfully, chances are, you will significantly increase your online conversion and minimise your website's bounce rate.

Now, though, with so many online channels, it's possible to talk to customers and prospects without always selling to them—which can actually help drive future sales.

Ways to Increase Customers Engagement online

1. Create an email newsletter

Whether you reach out to new leads or long-time customers, email is an effective tool for keeping in touch with them. That's why lifecycle email marketing should be part of your marketing strategy, no matter where prospects and customers are in the sales cycle. Create a blueprint for sending out emails at each stage of the sales cycle, from introduction to post-purchase follow-up. Send at regular intervals, but don't overdo it. And no matter the reason for the email, it must follow the next important step for increasing engagement.

2. Personalize your communication

You may not be able to name every one of your customers or know their purchasing histories by heart, but that should never be apparent in your messages.

Personalized emails and site content will not only catch customers' attention, but also increase the likelihood of a response.

Have an automation program in place, so you can populate messages with names, purchase details or other individual data. Make sure your data is up-to-date so the communication is relevant to the recipient and also fits their preferences for how they want to be contacted. These personalized communications will stand out among generic messages and make the recipient feel more appreciated—and, subsequently, more loyal.

3. Respond to each new interaction

One of the biggest complaints of today's digital landscape is the feeling that no one is listening. Too many customers have tried to solve an issue or ask a question via email or social media, only to get silence. As you can imagine, it's tough to feel engaged with a company that doesn't seem to care when you need help. Avoid this feeling by using automation tools to respond to every message and interaction that occurs on your site.

Set communication tools to respond in real time. Every time someone signs up for emails, submits a contact form, places an order, or sends a message to customer service, he or she should get an immediate response with a thank-you for reaching out and then a next step and call to action. Don't just respond to the outreach—use the response to keep the conversation going.

4. Ask for feedback

Marketing motivates action. That's why marketing messages always have a clear call to action that's easy to follow. The same principle applies if you're trying to increase consumer engagement. You read about responding to interactions in the step above. Turn those responses into requests for feedback. Follow up a purchase with a recap of the order, but also ask the recipient to send comments or concerns about delivery of the product or the product itself. Include rating and review tools on product pages. Give people opportunities to communicate with and about your business, and they'll take them.

5. Send out surveys

Listening has always been a part of marketing, which is why so many marketers rely on surveys to find out what customers and prospects want. In traditional marketing, this involved everything from phone and mail surveys to focus groups. Today, it can involve posting a survey on your website, on social media or sent via email.

Do you want to test out a new product or service idea? Measure consumer sentiment of your business versus your competitors? Create surveys (there are plenty of free online survey tools available) to get a sense of what consumers want. Make it easy for respondents to fill out and submit their answers, and encourage participation by offering incentives such as discount coupons or a chance to win a prize in a raffle.

6. Be active on social media

Consumers don't want to be sold to all the time. In fact, they're more likely to buy from companies that give them the information they want rather than the information companies want them to know.

Thanks to social media, you have the opportunity to reach consumers without being focused on products or past purchases. That's what makes it a great tool for increasing online consumer engagement. Post new content at least a few times a day to keep your feed fresh—and to keep followers engaged with your business.

...To get a different and a new result, try something new and different.

CHAPTER FOUR

Customer Engagement Metrics KPIs to Track and Measure

...be technical

Net promoter score (NPS)

A Net Promoter Score (NPS) is a survey that highlights customer loyalty and the potential for word-of-mouth recommendations. These surveys ask people how likely they are to recommend your product or service on a scale from 0 to 10. Based on their responses, you would divide customers into three groups:

Promoters: everyone who answered 9 or 10.

Passives: people who picked 7 or 8.

Detractors: all respondents with scores from 0 to 6.

You've likely seen NPS in action even if you've never heard the term. If you've ever been presented with a scale from 0-10 asking how likely you are to recommend a company, you've been NPS'd. The idea is that the most satisfied customers (those who rank you as a 9 or 10) will spread the word about your product or service.

When you survey your customers, some will say they'll probably promote you to their peers. Some will say they won't. And some won't feel inclined to share positive or negative information about you.

To calculate your NPS, subtract the percentage of survey respondents who would say negative things from those who would offer positive things about your brand.

Customer satisfaction score (CSAT)

A customer satisfaction score (CSAT) asks users to rate their satisfaction with a brand or one of its products. Usually, customer satisfaction scores are done on a scale of 1–10, with the option to write in additional feedback.

While customer satisfaction scores aren't a guarantee of people remaining loyal to your brand (or high spenders), they're certainly a strong predictor. In fact, McKinsey found that when a cumulative customer satisfaction score went up by one point, it corresponded to a 3% revenue increase. SaaS companies often measure CSAT by asking users for short one-to-five star or emoji ratings. You can use these quick check-ins to measure the customer experience with the features they use.

This is different from NPS, which provides a more general satisfaction rating of your product, service, or brand. In short, CSAT tracks customer satisfaction, and NPS measures customer loyalty.

Best for: Because they focus almost exclusively on new solutions and USPs, startups must measure CSATs. Small SaaS businesses need to know specific user preferences when offering suites of new tools. Larger companies need CSAT data when adding features but depend more on NPS scores for predictions.

Customer Effort Score (CES)

A customer effort score (CES) is a type of satisfaction survey that asks users to rate the ease of interacting with their brand on a scale of 1–7 (with 1 being the most difficult). A customer effort score can be used to measure the ease of everything from the ease of onboarding to their experience working with customer support to resolve a problem.

The goal of customer effort scores are – as the name suggests – to take away points of friction in the user experience, which could create a subpar customer experience (and block potential conversions).

Activation rate

Activation refers to the first time a customer gets value from your product or business. (It can also be described as their first "aha!" moment.) An activation rate is the percentage of users who've reached this milepost in a specific time frame compared to those that didn't.

Activation rates are important to track as they can set the tone for the rest of your customer relationship. If people don't quickly recognize the value of your product, they can start to lose faith in their investment. (Not to mention, low activation rates can point to a difficult-to-navigate interface or unsuccessful onboarding.)

And even though activation can be a slow-moving metric, it still packs a punch. In fact, at Segment we found that even a 1% increase in activation can grow to $1.5 million in annual recurring revenue (ARR) over five years.

Churn rate

Churn rate shows how many people abandon your service or product during a given time. Essentially, it's when someone stops engaging with your business.

Sometimes an opt-out metric determines your churn rate, like when a person un-installs an app. In other instances, a metric can be a strong predictor for churn: like a person who unsubscribes from your newsletter but continues to use your product.

Here's how to calculate churn rate.

Say you had 10 users at the start of your measurement period and 6 at the end.

10 - 6 = 4.

4/10 = .4

0.4 x 100 = a churn rate of 40%.

Feature adoption

Feature adoption looks at the percentage of users who interact with a specific feature of your product. This is an important metric as it relates to users' "aha" moment. That is, have they recognized the value of this new feature? (If not, expect customer engagement, and overall interest, to wane.)

Low feature adoption can point to a variety of issues that businesses can quickly work to rectify: from targeting the wrong buyer persona to software bugs that need to be fixed.

Feature usage

There is no pre-defined approach to measuring feature usage. Often you do this by looking at the percentage of people in your total user base who interact with a specific feature in a given period.

Feature usage can tell you which parts of your app or service deserve further development and which to consider removing. They can also signal when users are trending toward churning if their feature usage or visit frequency takes a dip.

If you notice a user hasn't engaged with your brand in a while, you can always leverage re-engagement campaigns to try to win back their business. These email or SMS campaigns usually consist of a few personalized messages that can flaunt your newest products and services, offer users an enticing discount, or serve up recommendations based on their past purchases or use of your product.

Benefits of Measuring Customer Engagement

By tracking customer engagement metrics, businesses can uncover opportunities to improve brand experiences and proactively avoid churn. Here are three benefits that you can expect from grounding your customer engagement strategies in data.

Setting better and more customer-centric vision and goals

Customer engagement metrics help businesses monitor what will ultimately determine their success: the value that customers are getting from interacting with your product or brand. Customer experience has become the deciding factor among consumers when it comes to choosing between competitors. And 75% of consumers said they're willing to spend more with a brand that nails it on the CX front.

By measuring customer engagement metrics, companies are able to have a clear understanding of how healthy their customer relationships are – and which areas of the business need work. This ensures that everything from product roadmaps to marketing campaigns are centered around customers' wants, preferences, and needs.

Improving your customer segmentation and experience

Customer engagement metrics are also a great tool for personalization. Customer engagement metrics tell businesses what customers find to be the most valuable (e.g. certain features they favor) and what they're interested in (e.g. listening to a specific genre or artist on Spotify).

With this information, businesses can create highly nuanced audience lists and tailor campaigns accordingly (e.g. the messaging or offers you send to your big spenders will likely differ from how you try to re -engage cart abandoners).

Developing employee engagement

On the flip side, high engagement rates among employees can be just as impactful for a business (and worth tracking). A Harvard Business Review study among senior-level executives found that 71% said a high level of employee engagement was critical to business success.

Engaged employees are more motivated and passionate about the work they're doing. By soliciting regular feedback (whether through manager one-on-ones, Net Promoter Scores, or surveys), businesses can ensure that employees feel empowered to do their jobs and have the autonomy and tools to do so, which contributes to the overall health of the business.

How to successfully measure customer engagement

Clearly define customer engagement goals

Every business will have different goals when it comes to customer engagement. And inside an organization, each team might be focused on their own metrics. For customer support, it could be strengthening NPS response rates, while the product team focuses on increasing active users.

However, a business should always have a "North Star" metric that all its subsequent goals are feeding into (something that's tied to customer value, and not just revenue). Aligning teams around this goal is the first step in any customer engagement strategy, as it answers the question of: what are we all ultimately working toward?

Don't skip qualitative data collection & analysis

Quantitative data like activation rates, churn, or product usage show what is happening with your customers. But it doesn't necessarily tell you why.

This is where qualitative data comes in. User interviews, focus groups, and customer support interactions offer direct insight into customers' emotions and motivations. As Segment's former CEO Peter Reinhardt wrote: "20 hours of great interviews probably would've saved us an accrued 18 months of building useless stuff."

Have a proper tracking system in place

Customer engagement refers to all the interactions and communications that take place between a business and its (current or potential) customers. In other words: it's a broad category.

As consumers switch between devices, and use more than 10 channels (on average) to interact with a business, having a complete view of a person's entire customer experience is tricky to say the least: 83% of companies admit they're unable to turn fragmented data points into comprehensive user records.

CHAPTER FIVE

Market share

...green and red light

A company's market share is the percentage it controls of the total market for its products and services. Market share is an essential metric for businesses because it's an indicator of a company's profitability and success. It can signal dominance in an industry and how well a company's revenue-generating efforts are working to achieve business goals.

Market share can affect operations, pricing of products and services, and, potentially stock market performance. A growing market share corresponds to growing revenue. That, in turn, means a business can scale up its operations and opportunity for greater profitability. To gain market share should be a serious business goal.

There are a number of strategies a company can put to work to increase market share. These include improving innovation, building and solidifying customer loyalty, employing a talented, dedicated workforce, acquiring other companies, deploying effective advertising, and pricing products and services efficiently.

A company's market share is the percentage it controls of the total market for its products and services. Market share is an essential metric for businesses because it's an indicator of a company's profitability and success. It can signal dominance in an industry and how well a company's revenue-generating efforts are working to achieve business goals.

Market share can affect operations, pricing of products and services, and, potentially stock market performance. A growing market share corresponds to growing revenue. That, in turn, means a business can scale up its operations and opportunity for greater profitability. To gain market share should be a serious business goal.

There are a number of strategies a company can put to work to increase market share. These include improving innovation, building and solidifying customer loyalty, employing a talented, dedicated workforce, acquiring other companies, deploying effective advertising, and pricing products and services efficiently.

Understanding the Benefits of Market Share

Market share is calculated by measuring the percentage of sales or percentage of units a company has in the overall market. Using the percentage of sales method, if a company has $1 million in annual sales and the total sales for the year in its industry are $100 million, the company's market share is 1%. Under the percentage of units method, a company that sells 50,000 units annually in an industry where 5 million units are sold per year also has a market share of 1%. Companies with high market share often receive better prices from suppliers, as their larger order volumes increase their buying power.

Increased market share and greater production go hand-in-hand, with the latter providing a company with the opportunity to decrease the cost to produce an individual unit due to economies of scale. Higher market share can help improve sales when existing, brand-loyal customers buy more of a company's products. Market share may also widen a company's overall customer base as potential new customers follow the lead of existing ones.

Gaining market share can strengthen and spotlight a company's reputation. In addition to boosting sales and increasing bargaining power, that can attract new, more talented employees.

How to Gain Market Share

One way a company can increase its market share is by improving the way its target market perceives it. This kind of positioning requires clear, sensible communications that impress upon existing and potential customers the identity, vision, and desirability of a company and its products. In addition, you must separate your company from the competition. As you plan such communications, consider these guidelines:

Research as much as possible about your target audience so you can understand without a doubt what it wants. The more you know, the better you can reach and deliver exactly the message it desires.

Establish your company's credibility so customers know who you are, what you stand for, and that they can trust, not simply your products or services, but your brand.

Explain in detail just how your company can better

customers' lives with its unique, high-value offerings. Then, deliver on that promise expertly so that the connection with customers can grow unimpeded and lead to new customers excited to join your base.

Highlight the advantages that your company offers customers that competitors can't match. Underscore your expertise in what you do and why that matters.

Create messaging that is focused, personal to customers, meaningful for those who might become customers, and actionable in a way that can achieve results for both the target audience and company.

The importance of market share lies not simply in maintaining your company's current share of the market. After all, as the industry grows, a company's market share must grow as well to stay competitive and profitable. Increasing market share is crucial and involves gaining a bigger share than you have already. That would indicate that your growth is greater than average and you're outperforming your competition.

Here are some areas a company can focus on to increase market share.

Innovation

Innovation that attracts customers can come in different forms. One is useful, new technology that a company develops, introduces, and continues to improve before competitors gain a foothold. Consumers excited about the technology buy it, use it, and can become repeat customers. Innovative technology can build a company's customer base with consumers new to the industry as well as consumers who leave another company for it.

A few other ideas for innovating to gain market share can include product innovation, production method improvements, and marketing strategies. The potential for high-value innovation exists throughout a company.

Customer Loyalty

Building and reinforcing relationships with existing customers by cultivating their loyalty is a smart strategy to gain market share. First of all, existing customer loyalty can help prevent customers from leaving a company for others when new products come to market. What's more, a company can broaden its base with the word-of-mouth marketing so often provided by satisfied, happy customers.

Take advantage of chances to engage with customers who desire a closer connection and to deepen their positive experience. An added benefit is that this organic opportunity to welcome new customers and increase market share often can come without specifically related increases in a company's marketing costs. Plus, loyal customers can sometimes share ideas for innovations to the products they love.

Skilled Workforce

A company that focuses on attracting and keeping talented employees is focused on increasing its market share. That's because skilled employees can become dedicated employees. That, in turn, can cut expenses related to hiring and training. Plus, a skilled workforce that excels at its tasks can allow a company to maintain its focus on producing exceptional products and sales. Attracting the best requires competitive salaries and a strong selection of benefits, including options for flexible work schedules and relaxed office settings.

Acquisitions

To win market share and dominate an industry, a company can consider buying its competition. Such a move actually offers multiple strategies to increase market share in one action. With an acquisition, a company takes a competitor out of the market and assumes its market share. It captures its customer loyalty. Moreover, it can put products, services, and other strategic opportunities already developed by its acquisition to work immediately. If a company can't buy another due to financial constraints, it can consider acquiring key employees to improve its own workforce and for the customer loyalty connected to those employees.

Advertising

Effective, frequent advertising offers a good opportunity to gain market share. Innovative branding and marketing through advertising can garner the attention of consumers, build connections with existing customers, and spur widespread desire for the products and services a company offers. High-impact advertising in different forms can help buyers understand and align with a company. No matter which advertising media is used, it's wise to maintain continuity across design, voice, and message to ensure a strong, positive, and lasting impression. Companies should also make sure that their advertising actually targets the right market segment for their products and services.

Price Reductions

Lowering prices is a solid strategy to help a company win market share. Lower, more attractive prices can attract consumer attention and loyalty. That can increase the all-important sales that drive market share higher. In addition to decreasing the actual price for products, a company can consider promotions, coupons, bonus items, and other customer benefits. For instance, incentives such as referral programs and free shipping can generate extra interest and added sales.

How To Prevent Loss of Market Share

To avoid losing its market share, a company should monitor its market share metric, keep an eye on the performance of its competitors, and take steps to improve the aspects of its business that can affect its market share standing. These can include things like product and service quality and pricing, customer satisfaction, the growth of its customer base, marketing, and advertising, the quality of its staff, and the potential for the acquisition of competing companies.

Increasing market share can be vitally important to the financial health and continued success of a business. A company has a number of opportunities at hand to, not just maintain, but gain market share. Every company should understand the value a strong market share offers and commit to the ongoing effort that it can take to build it.

CHAPTER SIX

Business Discipline

...the moral principles

Business disciplines refer to the practices that help a business grow. By putting a business practice into place, an entrepreneur can help ensure success and growth over the long term by creating a plan before the launch of an idea. Such disciplines help a business owner create a clear vision regarding the enterprise, set goals and create an action plan.

Business disciplines refer to the practices that help a business grow. By putting a business practice into place, an entrepreneur can help ensure success and growth over the long term by creating a plan before the launch of an idea. Such disciplines help a business owner create a clear vision regarding the enterprise, set goals and create an action plan.

Motivation And Personal Development

It is important for business owners to stay motivated and care for personal needs. Creating new personal and professional challenges can help an entrepreneur maintain his motivation. Increasing professional knowledge with industry-specific trainings and seminar can help him stay current and implement new practices.

Teamwork

Employees are perhaps the most important assets in a business, so it is important for a group to work in sync. By promoting and practicing teamwork, a business owner can take advantage of all the skills and talents within a team in order to raise productivity, quality and efficiency. Team-building activities can help ensure that employees work together like a well-oiled machine under a business owner's direction.

Holistic Bookkeeping

It is important for an entrepreneur to know how to manage her business' money. A business owner must always be aware of her business' financial situation and cash flow so she can remedy money problems at the source rather than treat the symptoms.

Creating A Vision And Plan

All business owners should have a vision, or a big picture, when it comes to an entrepreneurial venture. Creating a vision or objective helps provide a focus and a framework on which to base important business decisions. When developing a vision, an entrepreneur should consider the value he hopes the business will provide in order to formulate a corresponding business plan. Developing a business plan should help a business owner limit unforeseen circumstances so she is ready for any unplanned events.

Marketing And Customer Retention

Before embarking on or investing in any marketing campaign, a business owner should have a clear idea about the desired product. Every type of marketing solution a business uses should effectively communicate a clear message about a company's goods or services to the appropriate customers. When marketing, also consider ways to retain and satisfy current customers, keeping in mind that their needs and wants may change with time

CHAPTER SEVEN

Business productivity

...product is gain

Switching negatively impacts productivity; the employee view on task-switching is generally negative too. But automated email responses, data extraction, social media management systems and scheduling tools allow employees to focus on their strengths and not tedious to-dos, which ultimately leads to not just more productivity but increased morale.

Employee Flexibility

A happy employee is a productive employee, and one of the most important predictors of employee satisfaction is work flexibility. People like having choices and freedom, so provide it in the form of flextime, telecommuting options or simply more vacation time. This gives team members the freedom to choose how to be the most effective in their role while increasing employee morale. Even encouraging and providing time for self-care can improve workplace productivity.

The myth that employees can't be productive while working at home was effectively shattered with the COVID-19 pandemic. As many employees were forced out of the office, countless companies maintained or even increased productivity. Research from Gartner shows how even cutting out an office commute can boost productivity, so it's worth considering that kind of flexibility for your team. But if you're still concerned that home-based workers won't make enough effort, there is plenty of software that helps you track remote staffers' productivity.

No one wants to be just a cog in a machine, so encourage active learning and the development of personal and professional skills. Provide opportunities for employees to develop personal hobbies or to take on new professional duties. Back up support words with meaningful action. Offer to let a team member try a new responsibility for a trial period to see if they like it or give them time off to attend a work-related conference. Let them feel confident you're invested in their personal and professional development. These incentives can keep workers committed to your company and their responsibilities. Gallup data indicates employee engagement in the U.S. is in a slump, but reversing that can be a boon to your business's productivity.

Workflow Organization

Implementing an organizational system for tracking

employee responsibilities and workloads can streamline operations and make them more efficient. Such systems can help teams communicate regularly and effectively about long-term projects or goals. Scrum, for example, has teams meet daily to discuss their workloads from the previous day, the workloads for the coming day, and any impediments they face. These discussion points allow the team to sync on responsibilities and collectively find ways to overcome roadblocks.

By having your teams internally aligned and operating consistently, especially when part of your workforce is remote, you'll save time and resources that can now be spent on building healthy client relationships and completing projects. Workflow organization also decreases overlapping responsibilities and reduces duplicated work. Companies can even automate workflow organization to lessen the effort required for time-consuming tasks. An automated workflow allows employees to focus on strategic tasks requiring high-level thought instead.

Employee Development

Employees, as previously discussed, are most productive when satisfied and engaged. Staffers who fall into a monotonous routine will find themselves discontented, so it's crucial to engage with them and make the days feel less repetitious. No one wants to be just a cog in a machine, so encourage active learning and the development of personal and professional skills. Provide opportunities for employees to develop personal hobbies or to take on new professional duties.

Back up support words with meaningful action. Offer to let a team member try a new responsibility for a trial period to see if they like it or give them time off to attend a work-related conference. Let them feel confident you're invested in their personal and professional development. These incentives can keep workers committed to your company and their responsibilities. Gallup data indicates employee engagement in the U.S. is in a slump, but reversing that can be a boon to your business's productivity.

Natural Light

Don't think your office design matters? Think again. Providing access to natural light in the workplace can directly impact a person's positivity, with doctors at UCLA reporting that natural light improves mood and increases happiness. As established, this increased positivity impacts productivity in the long term.

Access to natural lighting in the office is an area where many U.S. businesses can improve. Take advantage of natural light by setting up desks near windows and removing obstacles that block the flow of natural lighting throughout your building. You can also encourage employees to get out in the sunshine during breaks for a boost from Mother Nature.

CHAPTER EIGHT

Business Management Theory

...the Henri Fayol theory

Henri Fayol is believed to be the founder of contemporary management theory which is drawn from his extensive experience in the management field. In other words, he is acknowledged for his contribution in the field of management, having established a foundation for modern management theory.

Despite the fact that the Fayol management theories were developed in the 1900s, they continue to play an integral role in modern society. For instance, the 14 principles of management developed by Fayol are considered the basis for management as witnessed in modern organizations.

In addition, he had set long term organizational goals which were: profitability, restoring confidence to shareholders, ensuring that the organization remained competitive, and maintaining the welfare of employees. All these activities which are based on the administrative aspect of management theory as applied by Fayol are part of modern management where organizations plan, set goals, and strategize.

Furthermore, organizational managers act as representatives of shareholders, set goals and plan how to execute the goals. As a result, most organizations have adopted these three activities to ensure the welfare of different stakeholders is achieved.

Profit maximization and gaining a competitive advantage over competitors are also major drivers of modern organizations which are pioneered by organizational managers. Although these examples are drawn from the mining sector where Fayol was the managing director and CEO, the perspective is still applicable.

Management in an organization leads to effectiveness and efficiency in the running of an organization. As noted by McLean, as the managing director Fayol emphasised a lot on what management entails, how it could be executed and how it could be applied to achieve effectiveness and efficiency.

In addition, he concluded by noting that the role of management was forecasting, planning, organizing, commanding, coordinating and controlling. This led to the development of different roles of management in an organization in order to achieve success and financial breakthrough or survive economic and financial crises.

As regards the element of forecasting and planning, a manager should be in a position to forecast and undertake an analysis of the environment in which an organization operates.

These managerial activities have continued to be practiced in contemporary management especially in the global markets characterized by high levels of change, increased competition, and increase in demand from customers.

Fayol gave organizations the managerial role of planning upon his engagement in managerial post. Planning and forecasting have since been adopted by organization in ensuring that they play an integral role in safeguarding the interests of different stakeholders.

He also held on the belief that it was the role of the management structure to organize different parts of an organization such as resources, organizational systems, infrastructure, services, processes, and procedures which ensures that an organization fully achieve its ultimate end goals.

Organizations are made of different players who have different skills such as managerial and technical skills. These two elements are part of the six activities which Fayol believed were crucial to organizational success. In this context, Fayol emerged as the first theorist to make a distinction between managerial and technical skills.

The distinction made was that employees at various levels within an organization required technical skills. This is because such skills would assist in the completion of different tasks in organizational levels. He added that even employees in management levels required a bit of technical skills which would be applied in the management of the production process.

On the other hand, Fayol's theory holds that managerial skills are important to employees who assume more responsibilities in managerial positions of an organization. The argument made here is that managerial skills are only necessary to employees who hold managerial positions while technical skills are important to all employees in an organization.

What emerges in this point is that despite the need for proficient skills to all employees, some skills are for all people in an organization while others are to be found in a particular group. This can be illustrated fully in the turnaround of Comambault where Fayol exhibited both his technical abilities as an engineer as well as a manager

The advantage of having technical skills is that a manager is able to use his expertise combined with managerial capabilities to effectively and efficiently run an organization.

Fayol has been credited for his role in developing the 14 principles of management. The 14 principles of management were designed solely with the objective of guiding a manager to undertake his/her daily managerial activities.

These principles have been designed in such a way as to assist managers in running successful organizations. One of the major principles applied in modern organizations is division of labour. Division of labour is used in reference to the distribution of work to different employees or groups so as to reduce the time taken by an individual or a group.

Based on this explanation, division of labour encourages specialization which reduces efforts for a group or an individual. In addition, division of labour develops familiarity and better work practices. The success of this concept can be drawn from Fayol application where he divided workers into different groups depending on their skills and expertise.

This improved the overall performance and reduced the

time taken in carrying out tasks. Division of labour in organizations encourages specialization which increases speed and level of performance.

Speed and high level of performance improves efficiency in the workplace by encouraging employees to perform more efficiently thus saving time.

In addition, employees are divided into small groups and the group elements are allocated job depending on their specialization and skills. The only limitation is that it leads to group identification which may have a negative effect.

Managers execute their obligation as custodians of the shareholders because of the responsibility and authority endowed in them. Fayol acknowledged the need for managers to have authority over others and show responsibility so that an organization can achieve its organizational objectives.

The implication made is that for an organization to

achieve its ultimate goals, managers have to exercise authority which comes with responsibility. Fayol gave the distinction between authority and responsibility and warned that authority should never be confused with responsibility.

Authority is considered as the power of an individual to give orders to a group of people. In addition, authority is used to exact obedience in the workplace which creates harmony and a better working environment.

Responsibility arises from exercising of authority over others in the workplace. Whenever a manager exercises authority to employees, different parties play their part in an organization. Managers have the responsibility to ensure that an organization operates smoothly. This can be achieved by exercising

authority over subordinate members of the organization. Note that managers play the role or coordinating activities in the workplace which is carried through the exercise of authority and responsibility. Some of the activities in modern management which require authority include harmonizing and unifying organizational efforts and activities. Despite the many benefits of the concepts of responsibility and authority, there are also disadvantages such as the abuse of authority and power by managers.

In order for employees to execute their roles without any hindrance such as strikes and stoppages, remuneration is deemed important. Remuneration emerges as one of Fayol's management principles, the management of an organization should offer a fair remuneration to its employees.

In addition, Fayol has described remuneration as the price an organization pays for the services rendered by its employees. In the modern organization, remuneration is paid in the form of salaries and wages. Furthermore, employees in any organization are paid based on performance or their level of value to such an organization.

Fayol goes to the extent of explaining that there are different types of numeration which organizations offer to its employees. The different types of numeration as stated by Fayol include non-financial and financial incentives, profit sharing, piece rates, job and time.

All these different forms of compensation play an integral role in an organization such as boosting employee's morale and motivating employees to increase their performance levels. Compensation should be fairly carried in an organization to ensure that all employees are satisfied.

Subsequently, harmony and understanding is achieved in the workplace which increases the level of production. Remuneration is used to stimulate individual employee initiative which plays an integral role in innovation and creativity.

Therefore, the principle of remuneration is often applied

by managers to carry out different tasks which may include other aspects such as personal satisfaction, self respect, and self interest.

A manager is charged with the responsibility of ensuring discipline, unity of action, and order in an organization. Observations that different departments have different functionalities which work harmoniously under the leadership of a manager.

In other words, managers play an administrative role as showcased by Fayol who was an administrator. Order and discipline are some of administrative management principles. Restoring and maintaining order in an organization involves organization and commanding people.

These activities revolve around the principle of authority. For a firm to attain prosperity, unity of command is carried out. What this means is that a superior should give orders to employees which should come from the ruling authority.

Fayol was keen to observe that dual command is more likely to result in conflict as it threatens stability, discipline, and authority. Although the term commanding seems more authoritative in the 21st century when applied in some organizations, at the time, Fayol used the term to describe the responsibility a manager has in leading and directing employees towards the achievement of organizational goals.

Organizations in the 21st century use the term leadership instead of command as meaning of the process of influencing, directing and motivating employees to execute their role to work towards the realization of organizational objectives and goals. All these are achieved through order, discipline and unity of action.

ABOUT THE AUTHOR

Insert author bio text here. Insert author bio text here

www.ingramcontent.com/pod-product-compliance
Lightning Source LLC
Chambersburg PA
CBHW070438220526
45466CB00004B/1733